Pierrot's Fingernails

Pierrot's

CANARIUM BOOKS ∘ NEW YORK, NEW YORK ∘

Fingernails

poems

Kit Schluter

MARFA, TEXAS · ATLANTA, GEORGIA · 2020

Canarium Books
New York City, Marfa, Atlanta
www.canarium.org

The editors gratefully acknowledge
Columbia University School of the Arts
for editorial assistance and generous support.

Cover & interior design by the author.

First Edition

Printed in the United States of America

ISBN 13: 978-1-7344816-1-7

Farai un vers de dreyt nien :

I'll write a poem about nothing at all :

GUILHEM DE PEITIEU

CONTENTS

PROEM (SKEUOMORPH)

It goes without saying that new work is the work that *"goes there." Still, for now, I've chosen to stare other suns free of their smoke…*

By degrees, then, tomorrow morning, I'll part my eyelids and squint through the flaming gauze of my headache, in order to tend to the concealment of my stupid datedness before you wake up.

Internal bashing will have become the unvoiced ritual of cornering myself in the salon of my body : a nightly break-in of a house that is burning, but only in the imagination of the burglar, whose hallucinations will have led him to pray beside my toilet, to wash his hands in its cool water, to scrub his face with my loofa, having entirely forgotten his intention to thieve.

There will be the planar scuttle of water rippling where my spit will have landed, just offshore.

And there will be the phrase au large, *which has always evaded my easy translation.*

And there will be bornes, *and* bornes, *and* bornes.

And there will be a quantity of unravished limbs.

But then, there will be no eponym.

BAD FAITH

I.

Into the bulbous crenelation of foliage I raise my star-shaped
finger. Without softness,
   the story perspires a sweetlessness, axillary as any latterday
bubo. Under my clothes, the skin coughs—
   it weeps a filthy amber, the color of overused motor oil.
Between myselves, one soul feels too plastic—
   but as long as there is at least a gust of light, there will be
some contour, some give, to the others.
   The natural world is lobotomized: its hair grows long,
turns to gold, falls away,
   and when my skull gets critiqued, rightfully, for taking
after centuries-old copper bells,
   it cracks under this stress in the atmospheric night.
   No matter which shrub I choose to lie in, I tend to find
another with binoculars tight to his eyes, fixed on
   some window, a body halted in its frame.

II.

What is an opulent form without a function: or, what is an adverb?

    What is the perfect use of the word *needlessly*, and what can I use to dowse for paranoia's nearest underground spring?

    I awaken to the possibility of my having no such hydrosphere,

        the brighter half of my chiaroscuro egging me to passive reception.

    There is no rhyme fit for my scream:

    my scream is ever petty, a sword-crossed, double chiaroscuro,

        a crosshatching of trusts.

    The normative is pedagogical,

        but only in high, high relief.

III.

I never skimp on the food I shoplift…
    but is there a name for slinking away from the inexpensive perimeter, like this, to the decadent aisles?
    And if a tree is named alone in a wood, can it be felled and dragged to the town square if no one's around to drag it there?
    There is nothing inconvenient about it, this disappearing,
    this falling away of the ground from which an argument gleans its blinding charm.
    I am an individual, thus I have no bedtime.

IV.

To derive my daily intake of sentencing from *ought*,
   my narrative scorn from *is*,
      I first consider illegibility as impossibility, then as joke,
subterfuge, and finally, as foil.
   In the interim, I consult my imagination—
   a vehicle, anyhow, hijacked by others...
      Landscapes are without end: nothing can be read, lest reading
become sacrifice.
   To rely too heavily on a single language:
   to cleave the interval between two.

v.

At the heart of the fingertip's whorl begins a mouth.
From this whorled mouth a cone arises.
At the base of this mouthed cone there wells up a pressure.
Out of this coned pressure eeks a thread.
With this pressurized thread is tied down a purple.
Under this threaded purple a garishness struggles.
Because of this purple garishness there clots a clotting
In this garish clotting a well is drying up.
And now, dangling in this clotted well:
a bag of urine in sunlight.

VI.

In an instant, I am going to tell you how I rely on things outside myself.

In an hour, I may have decided to lose myself to the steam instead.

In a day or two... how aberrant
this flipping and flipping...

Light that falls and sweeps my last anxiety out over the water from the cliff's foot.

The sand fanning out over the plague.

Lapsed, relapsed, prolapsed, eight to nine years away from that insidious basin at the foot of a waterfall,

in the heart of the crease denoting my opulence.

VII.

If I believe the concept of the ornamental would disappear given a minor adjustment of attention,
   it must be because I sense something essentially ornate in my own being here:
   a chain that ligatures a fire hydrant's cap
   to its open, bursting mouth,
   a flier depicting a face that can no longer be recognized as a face.
   Today I read of a name that resisted obliteration—the name as a site of paradise.
   And I read of the name as a frill, under a window in a labyrinth with a hot, soapy bath waiting at its center...
   All I ask of life is that it pose me in its question to myself— like that, my personality can only hit me at a glance.

I DARE YOU TO KEEP ME COMPANY

So you had me wait for you a thousand times over in the Rapunzel turret, where the deadbolt of the New World's last lock had been cranked into the passing mouths we had passively refused to liberate from the assembly line.

With a map you could seek the rift; I would meet you there, where the yellow seas curtsy to a vertical shore of mirrors.

I could have helped you banish the pines, but those voices, too umbrageous to be articulate, had already folded the sunlight like a topographical map, and it often grew too dark to see.

Thinking of obscure people in the community seemed to force them to coincidentally appear, so the flowers of a thousand lifetimes laid the way home, where the Cerbereans had kept our bedrooms just as we had left them.

Untying ourselves from those distant lives is not as deliberate an act as we thought it would be:

the motor is simply the process of forgetting.

COCAINE / ZEUGMA

That it is burning's capacity to kill that clues us into the feeding-unto-death occurring in the bush still astounds me, the bush being a thing water can touch, but which even the furthest extension of language cannot. As if the rejuvenating coolness of fresh water were an apology from the natural world as we drown in it, or rinse away the salt our bodies have perspired into our cuts.

But no one has ever drowned in fresh-water—only salt-!

(We, too, at the moment of our second coming, will turn away before appearing, like this implied presence of water, if for nothing more than to demonstrate the principle of zeugma to the still-pimply rhetoricians.)

And if a falling powder need some angle on which to momentarily rest, may it be a steep one, so most of it keep floating down into our nostrils. For the zeugma's is not a simplicity described by the cloud form—which would, in time, be determined by its washing away—, but by a centripetal attraction toward a space just to the left of our chests.

CONTE

At first the raindrops distributed themselves evenly over the clearing and the forest beside it (the eye could see no further), but slowly they spiraled inward toward the hand itself, as if streaming down the walls of a perfectly translucent funnel.

Rotating on the axis of its stationary wrist, the hand threaded a wisp of this matter out of the cloud's center, as if peeling the skin off a newborn by twisting the umbilical cord away from its navel.

A black dog emerged from the nearby forest and, sharpening her claws with a heart-shaped pumice, ran in circles around the hand, as if around a pit of spellbinding fire.

The cloud screwed into the palm and rang, *insofar as it grew denser*, like a champagne flute.

The palm expanded to the size of the clearing, and the fingers formed a wall, into which the dog collided, having been blinded by excitement as she rushed toward the forest whence she had come.

AFTER THE CANE SLIPS FROM THE CROTCH
OF MY NEWLY-PREHENSILE ELBOW

The slugs slugging across the doormat by the exit of the library call me toward their almost-Buddhist firewalking ceremony.

Their mucus trails (my aqueous humor) incant my right sclera on the tightly cropped black shag.

The appearance of their morphing antennae, like tumors and cysts that surge up, long and soft, merely to sink back under their pearskin flesh, confuses me, which only makes me want to touch them more.

But what I'm asking you is, when was it more pink than now—my eye—hot and dry with the choke-blue veins of undiagnosable crypto-iritis?

Two years ago? Two months? Two days?—Never?

Back when a good eye-gouging was still just a good eye-gouging?

No dress-up, then, just remorse, and bodily fluids:
interocular, sanguine,
precorneal, lacrimal, cerebral...

Through the empty sockets, a chrysalis of branches, warm only to a rougher kind of touch, strained into a novel form as I peeked in: the calf-and-knee corpus of generic pawns, some standing, some toppled, all scattered from the front row.

You held out to me a sorting hat brimming with slips of paper, folded and inscribed. Coleoptric noises snared up, grating from the fragrant, pulsing mulch, at six. Then longnecked trumpets rose above the rooftops in the square of thieves in liripipes and drag-clad gonfalonieres at eight-thirty, under sunset. That it was "sweat season in the golden lair," I only half-overheard from our swing on the holm oak.

Once our bower was filled with wildwood swine, and the bridebed full of blood. Though left these swine did we, gate open, to walk to town, leashed to our telephones. The neighbors chattered kindly to us over what they could not see. The satyrs, however, choked blindly on our garden's snug roots and wriggling croci. We agreed to pay attention and deal with the cold droplets falling from the awning over the market, the deep shallows, the growth, the mist, the grain, the sold, the sheet, etc.

I necessarily lightened my grip to breathe in melody—a one-step remove from ballad—still plump with the tendon broth of our knightly enemies, bow in hand. Seven years was I happily swathed and fed in a filial bower, and still I shied from walking over the peat of your own, for the silvering digested by its carbon sink.

ALONG A HIGHWAY, AT NIGHT

Where there is a living minx, there is a tower of meaning.

Along the base of the ocelot's eyelid inks up a glaucous crema.

Cranes cast no shadow, swimming through pools of sunlight.

Sometimes a chimp is given the right of way in figurative traffic.

Three guinea pigs equal one lightbulb on a table.

The starlings' crania are thinner than the dashes zippering the highway shut.

Prowling leopards hunger for the rosemary of Provence.

The pigs drink a maceration of cud and rain before the promise of shelter.

Cerebral impressions of collies terminate along the thoroughfare.

Elephants mourn the death of kin.

Siamese cats cling silently from the rafters of the bedroom.

The hopping toad's pads wetten bread crusts in the Alps.

The cinema does not admit a bonnethead shark.

The owl's gaze is sanguine.

Now and then the eel opens her eyes along the way.

A bat hangs naked beneath the sheer bedding of its wings.

A tractor would descend fatally, if into a giraffe's throat.

The likelihood of a lion surviving cancer is zero.

The cockatiel's eyelids are likened to an aviator's goggles.

The koala meets a crustacean burdened by rare shame.

To enter the chamber through which one must pass, the skin should be soft and appropriate to be fashioned into leather. Remove the hair in waxed strands, and lace the body's enclosures shut with this twine.
We say the same of the sky, its patchwork of amorphous signatures.
To find oneself beneath this sky is to close it with its own appendages, its thumbs of rain that extend from the center of its palm, to recognize a voice but see a different body.
That's a dark horizon : as in, where are you moving toward?

That I am willing to gather for you living flowers, and yet I bathe in a tea of others dead,
　　plunge in their statements, again and again…
Let us look at the sky we once had, but tentatively, where yellow fingers meet, and
　　strange, wet slits rain down rain down until the trees, when sawed, collapse
　　like dollops of rice pudding—and let us regard this sky,

we its unloosed product, and follow each other's glances as one follows
the eyes of a cat stalking a dragonfly caught between two windowpanes.

☆

Empty rays sent out as feelers come to a new ground, illuminate the air that hangs in swabs above the grass—these we call salutations,
each a day horizontally extended over sleeping bodies that twitch in sync with their dreams,
a fate of high-cast words packed down in a canon that, someday, will no longer respond to this gunpowder.

☆

And does a shadow age as it grows longer, as when,
beneath a setting sun or a low full moon, the head elongates to the size of the chest,
the legs to the height of the entire body,
and beneath each planted foot there forms a darkness
the very size of the fetus from which they, eventually, sprung?

The hours surge away. By force of an unforeseen gravity, they retract into their turbid centers.

We alone are responsible for this recession, and so we find ourselves in its midst; it attracts us into a space of untruth when we speak.

In this silence, we lay our gratitude down gently.

There is an earth we cannot walk upon, for it is covered with our descriptions of it, from which blooms a distracting foliage.

There are truths you do not believe.

There are angles of passing time that house you and cause you to retract like the hours.

One smells the infinite here, in the morning before one has awoken, where one must deny what one believes in light of what one knows to be true.

Must this series be resolved, or may I wait here to be scattered again by the concerns of the sleeping?

Perhaps our frailties, as opposite extremes, must converge, and thus would we ignore the long periods of silence endured, and ascribe them to the faults of the days in which we rest and surpass each other's edges.

Without regret live those who would burn for the lies of a stranger.

From these heights it is unclear that it is us whom we are watching.

From behind, a precipitate of voices listens to the morning, complete, which bathes me in its teachings, and this I call night.

As the sun rises, it extends into the morning as a hill into the sky, discrete and singular. Haste works patiently upon us, the haste of the morning to conceal itself within a novel form of the day's evolution.

Its language may be foreign, but in its repetition a parallel sense precipitates.

Continue pulling those bows across your throats and I will follow you into these new attitudes that speak from morning and break through the darkness of their sources like the shoots of a crocus.

I extend to you the crescent of the spine, and attend this body that hangs like lightning glass from angles of conversation.

2009

TRUST

When I first looked in the mirror, I thought I looked dead, but I had simply become a child.

Beside my face was a blue cake so radiant, even its light was edible.

THIRSTY BESIDE THE FOUNTAIN

There is no general interest in the rehabilitation of those deemed useless; and the supposedly good only get strung up by one ankle—slipped blades to hide under their tongues.

It takes no more than a city's reflux to burn a man,
and you really are smelling what you're afraid you're smelling.

In the fallout shelter there will be no more singalongs, no air to feed the fire—just a phosphene singed on the back of your eyelids, and writs...

writs! flitting toward you while you recline and drink,
a half-empty bottle standing upright in your fathomless crotch.

COIGN OF VANTAGE

Take my word for it : the salty blue sphere is the most laughable
shape in all of geometry
   because, when its shadow arrives, mopey at the threshold,
   an unaccompanied poetry spills out—
   but it's all been said before,
   on a broadside, in luscious, azure paragraphs
   where clause after clause apportions ethical contemplation in
a fantasy so habitual
   tears of laughter stream from a fuzzy drupelet of blue paint
   as I eavesdrop on the four older men holding court at the
round table
   as their words turn to pollen, clouding out their mouths
   with the tedium of explaining the difference of a 0 and an O
to someone who has never before seen the Roman alphabet.

FAREWELL, JACKSON C. FRANK!

After all the toxins were purged with fasts,

after all our grandfathers were glimpsed naked in their windows,

after all that's been brought to light by reported sightings of unicorns and Bigfoot,

I finally understand: you never did love me.

But this time, it's not a matter of piecing together the half-buried wreckage of some antediluvian arc, nor of rocking an illegible booklet to sleep in a crib... not even of closing my eyes just that much tighter.

No, it's the same old story of the widowers, the toxins and the fasts, the avian holes in the trees, the woodpecker, the hummingbird and the oriole, the California grackle, the Louisiana perch and the tuna in the sky, the sun with wings, the gilled moon, the hearsay asleep on its mat and the... the, the, the...

It's not a piece of gossip supple enough to woo a captive audience, but the gun at our backs: the food on our families' plates.

(But is it not also the little room where we're forced to hose each other down after dinner, at whose window the morningbird never stops to sing?)

SUMMER !

Dreams until now were futuristic, slices from a fruit almost ripe,
or with the hair on my skin comes the grating that contains me.

A window at garden-level with dull moonlight and three
pieces of unbuttered bread, like glass dipped in water,

disappear. The light knitting a spherical grid leaks
from your tear ducts in icicle forms. No, I'm there for no one,

and every time you think suicide is on deck, sweet summer
arrives with its play of intensely bright shadows, vague and
  obsolete.

INCLUSIVITY BLUEPRINT

I. IS FAR / IS BLUER

Now alone, I've lost access to that "redemptive" escape,
the open and the concealed have swapped spirits,
and by law you are on a high shelf of transition,
looking down on the upcast eyes of the city
milked over with the glaucous stuff of in-between grounds.
And by law this can't be sadness, but
that something out at the point where adjectives fail.
I don't know what to call it : unwilling?
My attentions drift to spaces that feel
at first aesthetically conservative,
though you have given me
this extension of your person,
and within it I recognize
beneath the novelty
the shapes I first learned to inhabit :
lines straight or arcing,
simple forms, like triangles, quadrilaterals, hexagons, etc.,
and inside, perspective too still follows its old patterns
(what is far is bluer)
which is to say that space is the same as ever,
and this time it's not a matter of touch, but sight.

But remember. You are only here as a process,
as a space a material forced out of its native structures
can return to
when the stakes get raised
even one notch too high.

II. INCLUSIVITY BLUEPRINT

The point is to lock your jaw, glass, and screen,
To make them less like windows, portals less confessional,
To slant their roofs and ceilings, be they sinking or rising
Through canals of futurity with loss as peripheral banks.

Farewell and good-bye, between these words a choice,
Quantities of desire, almost a flavor, whether to rear up
Image or flesh, or, if you don't believe my mistrust,
Watch the Imitation Spring crying snow on the shoots

And my choice to view hindsight as pedagogical
Has locked me out of your inclusivity blueprint,
But into our already-superabundant hoarding chamber,
Where joy becomes indistinct and more meaningful,

A vague ease in roundabout yet concrete forms.
So I grow this warm counterpart to time's accordion,
By turns inert and volatile; you turn away
When you smile, it's infectious, that modesty in light,

But happiness too can be difficult to trust outdoors.
Time and again without a roof it floats away.

III. THE CITY THEY GAVE YOU

On another earth, the parents who love you are walls.
Beyond them, you can see the city—the city they gave you.
At my edges you are lonely. Let me blur them:

> *break/fissure—rupture/urethra*
> *caption/nimbus—mackerel/opus*
> *sanctus/rage—bleat/now*
> *frozen/like—prolonging/jaw*

They gave you no city. Let me blur them:

> *voice/upset—voice/centered*
> *layman/abstract—another/body*
> *unforeseen/plastic—freight/heat*
> *astringent/committal—narrative/hope*

They gave you no city. Let me blur them:

> *salmonella/healthy—desire/cóntent*
> *imprévu/because—elsewhere/no*
> *sequence/derision—cancellation/bi-polar*
> *jokes/sleep—nard/burial*

Let me blur them because, good as they've been to you,
they gave you no city:

breakage/point—return/confess
soak/loin—creak/moan

pure/joy—light/because
unanimous/forge—agree/forget

You knew that's how it would end,

agree/forget

But I didn't mean to write that there.
It was you who meant me to.

The smell of mint, smoke, and smothered candles stolen
from a highway memorial,
  and slow-burning red lights, rotating in the golden throng
of elsewhere's crickets,
    approach like a strange animal in the dark brush.
  Rustling bodies, supine beneath a triangle of stars, previse
arrivals,
    the approach of one segment's ending and another's begin-
ning.
  They seek the waning Pleiades, which no longer illuminate
the coupled nights
    constellated throughout the vegetable garden.
  As if spitting our images onto film, they synchronize their
movements
    with the conductor's wand of these first breaths of autumn
    to find the narratives concealed by the overflow.
    But you mustn't say never, mustn't say a thing,
    lest you spoil the dream of becoming a bird,
    and having access to these secret plains of basilica.

And once the traces of significant events appear to have been
swept away,
    where your vision and its blankness wait around the corner
    in the shadow of the rain that widens more gradually
    than the smoke of images here left unchosen
    for the vagueness of their Fibonaccian expansion,
    where I learn a lesson,
    where I undergo changes imperceptible until I return to
the foraged nest,
    where I find myself begging you to return to the habits by
which you were once identifiable,
    where I lurch apprehensively toward our friends,
    whom I mistrust for their capacity to steal you, whom I
love by keeping still…
    —I know. I hope to change and not waver
    beneath the impossibility of remaining tangible.
    If only the heart, as a fruit, were yours to consume.

VERGANGENHEITSBEWÄLTIGUNG

To never age
To never be alone

Before until
During since

After toward
Within beyond

The terrifying horizontality of water

Fingers reach out of the bushes and tickle me, while the exhalation of fish bubbles up like raindrops falling upward out of the water.

First a revolution,
later a holiday,
later the bank buys back the blood.

My heart has turned into an egg carton, grey and tough, housing all these yellow, transparent things that smell awful if they don't get used just as soon as they break.

The last thing I'd want to be is a copycat suicide, but if my body were to jump out that window, who would be able to stop my sight from crossing the threshold first?

And if then, my body, having stopped itself for fear of this kind of imitation, were to feel a breeze, teetering there, thirteen stories high,

but felt no resolve to turn back in, where the impossible length of life washes over us with the cadence of waves— and possessed no will to take the plunge...

Rain, rain, go away.

The sun is so revivifying!

How it sharpens the edge of our cognition, or rather, sculpts its central precision miraculously out of a fog, which, in time, is revealed to be composed of fruit flies,

which, in turn, must be trapped and drowned, like me, in this wine...

I didn't expect to take on the form of the pregnant body
waiting out the gradients of a narrative
   standing lightheaded from suddenly feeling tall,
   when what had once been luminous and discrete felt more
like sculpting a quiet afternoon
   whose minor passages like namesakes converged.
But it's marvelous to fall *pre*-you, to realize *bi*-you, to
suspend *semi*-you, to curtsy to *mega*-you!
Still we settle for the under-thrown and its verb every
time, in order to find a face irreducible to plaster,
   and still, you have to choke it off the more you think of it,
   choke it closer to connecting two hollows
"where you are necessary
I cohere," even when embroidered and the lips are closed
after a crosswind.

As soon as I told myself I'd finally come back to the moment after all these unoccupied years, I was an hour into a fantasy of remembrance:

of fireworks, of baculitic flares, ashen but petaled as rose

cinders of ghosts left ghosts pulled in by droves of fingertips laid across the sky's harp.

Frigates loom beyond the sand.

Decked eyes founder, crank inward toward the spectacle.

Life must be watched closely, as Queen Anne's lace picked apart and flicked to the wind.

1.17.—I come back to write with face set against the phantasm of genius one more time, dreaming it has a false gravity, like moving day. The weight of an hour of change. I don't speak on behalf of anything more than vaunting. No, because this is a fish with milkier scales, a given *enjeu* with a hysterical structure. It's gritted teeth, a pale *petite mère* all dopey from fishing, a hungry and quartered pedagogue, death, the doubled monsters and morons from Batmacumba. No, it's more the terrifying side of tropicalism, terror-tropicalism, mopey and determined to be so. My teachers work in detached ways with eyes on the life-giving bodies; on the letter, on the leg, on the eight teeth excavated at twelve.

1.18.—Listen, Judas. Before you get out of here on bail, death will have soaked us up entirely. Everyone showed up with a dry sense of humor and tubes of Jergens. The table's legs, their war with the wind. A boon to collect them one by one and proclaim it a scandal. To say so without being heard. To warm up to the hanged, say, "I want you." Fanatical indifference of the eye in you now.

1.19.—I return from where I've done a few somersaults in order to hear your voice on the phone. Uncertain. Sometimes I hate myself, and brutally. I am beginning to seem like an ingrate. *No, Pedro, I don't want to whitewash* puta *out of the text, but I will picture something else there, (some kind of knife), so light can cover me with its soggy feathers.* I consult the pool boy, *What hour is it? What minute?* I have to translate for him. I circle, sobbing, the blood red lightbulb. Burning with waiting. Transistor radio. Polaroid. Blue passport. Blue sky. I earn my keys with one thousand one hundred fourteen somersaults on the balcony, a descort sung in the park. I stick a pin into the blue waves of China on a map. Fearfully, I stick a pin into where the venerable Li Po once lived. I shoo the movie about him out of my eyes before the conclusion (a given at this hour): he did not commit suicide because of his revelations. Rather, he was on the brink of falling, when an angel who once sold him cast iron wares seized him with the contagious and electric fury of battle. I lose hope and grow as old as four stars combined, as the commander's entire flotilla almost tattooed on the captain's foot.

1.20.—Everything I never said to you is between these margins. (A curious consolation.) The jump toward was always another thing entirely. A snoop is never directly informed. Jealousy is a theater : the time of voice subtracted from a number without unit. The postcards. When they arrive. Certain silences, never anything more. I exceed the varied attentions of the bowing heads. I'm *risking my red lapis* by getting into this debt. Arrive now. Today, here, suddenly, from the proposition, from the stick, I read *New Tales* in braille. Three variations on erasing a signature. Three days for the checkbook from the agency. I send the agent away, I cross-dress. Happiness is half the transport. Leaving the cinema hypnotized. The escalator and waiting and the escalator and waiting, in this empire, but I am going to burst into tears. Before this, sustenance : pushing in. Listen : *How these enchanted waters gush . . .* It's still beforehand. [Waits.]

1.21.—You will always be able to touch me in this memory, but don't ask me now for the respect I could only give when living half-logically. A lake of stone, livid and erect: these are my funny angry faces. I cry tears of Chanel, passing my hand along the guard rail, perfectly horizontal, in Cherbourg. But this is somewhere else now, or has a different name. I miss my teachers, am waiting at the glass station. Water. A postcard never lies: I *will* see you again, being male and from another continent. Touching me: let that be your shortest response, without words that speak beyond forgetting, in a murmur. And what else? You don't want to know the other woman, so what good am I, with my chest puffed out in front? She instructed me: said longing is a form of repulsion ("one of the three stations of water"), for it takes account of this very object, bright and without name.

1.22.—*Travelling [sic]*: Late, the night my new housemate gets in. Everything in its right place. I have hidden all the papers I have ever written on. I confirm, for my own good, my ability to assist him. Never again will I speak a word to you. From high in the mountains of Petropolis, in a boating cap and raincoat, Elizabeth reconfirms : Loss is more difficult than never having had, or ... I take back out all the papers I have ever written on. Your gaze I scrutinize, not your body. In perfect, simultaneous translation, my hands trembling : *É perigroso*. In the Kodak photograph, Carolina. The voice far off in the mountains, an undispersible fog of passion. The voice against the mirror that is my two eyes, contradicts itself, as if it were itself two grumpy travelers. The voice eviscerated by the walking speeds of three babies : it could really make you throw a fit. I will never say another word to you, I repeat. I need it to be late, very late in the night, so late that I myself become misaligned (by poverty, by thirst), haunted by the revenants I see in this endless night : without such a light appearing even one more time. The confusing light of my endless day.

SUBTERFUGE

When first studying Romance languages, the student will often remark how sexist that the adjective describing a group of 99 women and 1 man calls for the masculine. *La, la, la…* This is undoubtedly true. *La, la, la…* But later, oh the joy! *la, la, la…* when this student, having mastered the language, commits the subterfuge (whose possibility must have been embedded in the tongue by some deep-seated, unaddressed desire of its male grammaticians) of applying a feminine noun, such as *une personne*, to a man, and so forces the world to refer to him, in deference to this word, with feminine adjectives. *La, la, la…*

COOCHY-COO

You can call me *Puppy*, or you can call me *Sweetybuns*.

You can call me *Glasscake, Cromagnonpoops*, or *Pigeonswelter* …

You could even just click your tongue twice whenever we catch eyes—

ah, from no matter how far away …

but whatever it is you choose to call me (*Coochy-Coo* would do)

know I'll gut it out,

and all these names will become uniform, suddenly, under this dumb excitement always welling up inside me …

That name is mine, yes, more so than my given name,

because the one I adore gave it to me …

To be named again, correctly this time, with this name I trick myself into believing I've been waiting for all these years …

(Silly, silly man.)

The other night I was out with three friends, when we started talking about the phrase "to have something under your belt."

One thought it had to do with the genitals : mastery as absorbing a subject into the flesh of the labia, sucking a material up the straw of the urethra.

I thought it had to do with stashing knowledge at the belt line, as I've seen certain friends do with books, at the base of the back or against the underside of the belly.

Another thought it had to do with dominance : understanding as the whip you crack upon what, before, you hadn't had under your control.

The last friend only said one word, "digestion :" learning as the consumption and subsequent processing of a metaphysical food. (After consulting a few sources, his seems the closest fit to the common historical understanding of the metaphor.)

PARAPHRASE OF MARX

Buoyed up by society at large, I foresaw that in my times of leisure I would continue to practice the arts by which I have successfully resisted definition. Then the day came when a single question disturbed this course of action to which I had disposed myself: on whose back am I reclining while I set these afternoons aside for navel-gazing?

With no end in sight, the formlessness of my personhood had become undeniably masturbatory, masturbatory in an absolutely negative sense: a masturbation that yielded no pleasure and, at the moment of climax, did not liberate me from, but united me with, the deep anxieties of the global violence over which I realized, too late, I had been coming.

THE APPLICATION

The object of my application was to gain access to a plane of language honest yet completely discursive. Like a procedural work, it was meant to provide me a strict framework to liberate me from my intuition and habits, gracefully stultifying the products of my free-range creativity with its stringent demands.

The application taught me of economy: I desired a new, terser voice. I filled it out, again and again, as nothing more than a literary exercise. As it restructured the interests and aims of my writing, and then my very manner of speech, I admired its austerity.

The application taught me English. It forced me, in fact, to learn English all over again. Its questions served as a model for the English I hoped eventually to speak.

But when they offered me a job, I knew I had done something wrong. I looked back and wished I could read the application for the first time again, repeatedly, one time after another, applying alive and in death, a virgin applicant filling out its form for the first time, forever, and ever. And when I heard myself say yes to their offer—O god, only now can I see the irrevocability of my mistake...

Don't talk to me.

This would be easier were I made of glass.

TOWARD BECOMING LITERAL

To kill the movement toward becoming literal, I built this excuse for expression to speak to you in secret of my autoimmunocentric desire to just give up and let my spirit rot in codependence with my sacroiliac joint. For if what I tell you were to get back to ears craving anonymity, the ungenerated skin cycle would be made to leave town, the way I warn would become an instance of lore, in movements of anatomic wax ring toss.

Part of me thinks I should say it all, flesh it out to the extreme, but then, looking back … to have gone home the other night, Notebook—I swear! To have been that reckless mess in that traveling counter-public event, then clerical, then obedient, and only then could sleep, and only lightly because brightly I loved the hypergrammatic intent tower, the super-brand-new garden of continuous charades, the absolute comfort of it all. What an arm extended between us, suspended in whiskey! (An orb, too.)

I see now how much easier it is to abstract every last thing, but more softly, apologetically -phobic of emo sewage wrangling the derelict lingo, instead of a cogent motive to be treated with a dignity manifest only in subsequent editions—not in prelapsarian time.

The measure of stride, first with, then without friends. Waiting out the shelf-life of these stumped, disappearing gestures toward killing reason itself. For extreme amounts of writing are an oppression of speech, and I am not to speak to you of the censorship and divorce present in my daily routine, nor am I to think of you when I sit alone or wake at night alone, feeling empathy for book and self for want of drafting. Not accompanied, nor am I alone; I am with you, so I am out of season.

I have somewhere surely lived a toy life with your epic cycle of slow remediation, while firs on the gum tree warped into these hyperbaroque limbs, these adamantine vessels losing foreignness beneath the same blossoms.

To remove a part of my body, to become someone else in a public state, we too camp out in this parking garage and increase the unilateral carnage of our almost parallel lives. Our place is under the initially private highway, where the archangel Gabriel doesn't touch us, damaging our cheek bones, or mark us elegiacally. It isn't as complicated or clean as you originally thought, but functions like one solid receptacle, this being stuck here in the anxiety of letting go of the wheel, going 90-something, this desire to halt my adaptation to the sequential derision of bipolar cancellation. (I didn't know it would seem so historic to be conscious of my pulse.)

The daytime hesitations that provide this o.c.d. analysis of specifics its raison d'être are actually harder to justify than just going out and staying out, as "a social appendage who is also drunk."

I used to think the body a landless metaphor for the scriptural right to territory, but there is no guardian anymore. And when it's time to leave the gazebo, will I finally achieve non-eternal life? And again, if we're so misled by majoritarian phylogeny, why do we instinctively people the dominant?

I asked the 8-balls, the talking mirrors, the tarot cards, the fortune tellers, the flower torn leaf by leaf, the horoscope, my intuition on drugs, and they all replied alike: "In order to have a lot of light ones now lonely with the fan on, caught in indulgent self-reflection too graphic for the dragon cherub."

ILLEGIBILITY

Watch the better days riding their magic carpet up through the windmill arms!

PIERROT'S FINGERNAILS

*Eunuch Pierrot's feet are constantly shifting. He digs his big toes into
the soles of his shoes to a rhythm determined by the objects around him :
gaps in foliage, passersby, signage along the boulevard. He takes
tiny steps forward, his back hunched. His arms hang loosely in their
shoulder joints, but go rigid at the elbows. Eunuch Pierrot's knees rise
high and flop to the side of his waist as he walks. His head pecks back
and forth like a street pigeon's, but he knows he mustn't—absolutely
mustn't—bob his head up and down. He moves shyly to a double-
time drum, which only he can hear.*

I want to castrate the impotent and double-castrate the
eunuchs
 and Pierrot,
 Pierrot as he sings this, the softest of light—
 you must know the extent of his impotence. One evening,
on a subway car, facing me, a clown
 thin as a boiled fingernail hiding his spindliness in an
embarrassment of an outfit. He was trying to leave nothing
 behind—at most a slug-trail of humor—to disappear, in
this subway car, his legs willowy and hands lithe for the
miming. And to everyone around him, he had, in fact,

already disappeared, undone, even, the very fact of his birth.

His nose, fine as his little finger, and more so ; his eyes, prettily crowfooted under the paint, from wincing or smiling
(the smiles in company and the winces, alone, always alone).
But he was, in his own right, ambitious—
his impotence was ambitious, and excessively so.
He would look down at his feet, as they walked ahead of him, like an old widow walking her lap dogs.
His ambition was plain :
like a thumb it drove his head down through his neck and into his chest, from where he would peer out at the world through the porthole over his heart.
I look at him there looking at no one,
and think back on something you once said of his writing :
the content is radically free, but the form, it's totally straightjacketed. You wondered at this libertinage
choked out through clenched teeth :
It made perfect sense, seemed rather
closeted to me.

There is an aesthetic object, the terms of which are determined by Pierrot. Is there a legitimacy to the struggles it voices?

For Pierrot to speak in anything but the terms of his privilege is for Pierrot to express himself in bad faith. The sole way for Pierrot to express himself in good faith is in absolute decadence. Pierrot encounters his good faith only when expressing ornamental thoughts.

Any aesthetic object made by Pierrot is ornamental to the subaltern discourse—the true discourse—in which struggle may be expressed in good faith. There is no space for struggle in Pierrot's writing. I don't care if this sounds severe, it is not: let him cry in silence.

Poetry is useless to the extent that Pierrot is its poet.

Pierrot wants to know how his language will appear to change if he, as now, holds his face very close to the paper and writes very slowly, concentrating on the inscription of each letter:

will it produce a more thoughtful text?

Sometimes, when he writes without premeditating his subject, he is more or less cracking his knuckles: it brings, at least, a similar satisfaction.

But when he writes like this, errantly—

with his cocked head far from the writing surface and his arm at nearly full extension—

his handwriting and the meaning behind the words it represents suffer a twin carelessness.

That he will keep his face so close to his notebook that he can smell the wet ink of his pen is his resolution—

that he will write more slowly, too, taking in the shapes as each letter palpates its way into form. But when he moves

his face away from the page:

vertigo! the table rising,

the way a horizon conveys sideways beneath a still sky after one has watched the ground outside a moving vehicle.

Pierrot, what did you suppose would be there to approach?

Pierrot speaks from the gulf behind his forehead.

Seen from above, his skull is a labored, though perfect, circle;

a height from which it would be, gravitationally, impossible to fall;

unsuturing tongues, as the lover parts.

That one's given name cannot be changed without bending the law is the birthplace of fiction.

Pierrot's struggle is that he has no transcendent struggle, but doesn't believe in a literature of leisure. This pins him into a corner

from which no one, including himself, wants to hear a peep.

For fear of taking up space, he writes into hollow after hollow,

rather than build structures to inhabit.

(Were his writing a city, it would be an encampment of poorly-laid foundations and half-constructed walls.)

And once, he felt so afraid of words that he wrote fewer and fewer of them, though the pressure of their containment inside him became dizzying.

Pierrot's pen is writing poorly, so he opens it, suspecting the ink must be running low.

No such thing: it's been a month since he replaced the cartridge, and it's still three-quarters full.

His pen doesn't falter for running dry—but for underuse, for the ink of all the words he hasn't written, now encrusted upon the nib.

Jubilant Pierrot skips on his toes with his center of gravity shifting from side to side. He holds his hands on his hips while he prances, giggling without end. This is his most expressive state, but seems to occur less and less with age. He now understands it to be his most polarizing comportment. Often, as he skips along, he can be heard exclaiming—so quickly, the words can hardly be understood—"Che bello! Che bello! Che bello! Che bello!"

Eventually the only thing left to do is stop writing, when the hand holding the pen has grown numb, waiting for permission to write.

Even a misplaced ear can't unhear what it had no permission to hear.

The bedside table has been polished. The choice has been made to look over no one's shoulder but his own:

to retreat, slowly, from himself.

Occasionally Pierrot happened upon a more *gallant* party that recalled to his mind the semen-scented lindens of Tivoli and the soft, tumbling

light, and *being seventeen* in Toulouse when springtime was
finally come, and that anybody could have stayed home on
these lovely nights
   seemed impossible, the whole city having streamed out
onto the streets to sit before the open air *cafés* or
   pig pile on the rolling grass along the *promenades*, and even
when no one
   seemed to believe in his happiness, and his song was mingling
with the moonlight *bathing* Tours, he would, *bock after bock*,
   empty whole pouches of tobacco in single nights—
   half down his own windpipe,
   half doled out to the handsomer men among the strangers
he had only just met,—
   and all of this under lights which looked increasingly like
stars strung through the trees at the *guinguette*,
   with his black-capped head, comet-tailed and wrenching
   in circles, downward,
   among the falling globes of blonde light
   drawn against unclearly-located vertical
   crimson surfaces, and the sky wasn't deep then, but *purple*,
   so thick and soft, and lower than usual,
   low enough he might even reach up and spin a warm
cocoon of this *cotton candy* around his open hand as a gift for
one of these *strange* new men...

but he willed himself to forget all that, to forget
the color of his skin beneath its paint, which fell away, like
any color from his body,
almost mathematically ; but the high-pitched, falling saw
waves of light could not be
removed from the surfaces they fell upon—
only *bocked out*, in groups of three or four,
lyrically,
almost sarcastically
slow.

Let me watch you tie the laces of your slippers, Pierrot, so I
can see the muscles work
under your forearm. Let me graft distraction onto this
boredom,
so the fruits of one bear the other's seed.
Without a full-length mirror, you have to stand on the
edge of your bathtub to view your whole outfit in the little
looking glass above your sink.
No use in reading the writing of the indolent :
the hinges linking its images break away, the transparency
of its windows, occluded by dust.

Big Bad Pierrot walks with chest puffed and spine awkwardly stiff. His head tilts slightly downward atop his straight spine, and pivots like a sclerosed joint. With each step, the balls of his feet fall toe-first, and his knees snap backward ever so slightly. Big Bad Pierrot maintains a lower center of gravity than any other Pierrot. He assumes this posture when he wants to achieve the feeling of invisibility.

Is the reason Pierrot doesn't have any poems to write that he
doesn't think about poems throughout the day like he used to
  back when they really mattered to him
  back when the poems he wrote taught him how to live
  like a user's manual written in his own saliva
  when his poems were edible and succinct
  dense as the night
  and they staved off hunger and jealousy
  and let him know what it feels like to understand himself
  to have a purpose
  to bloom under the light of his own sun
  no
  this poetry is dead
  dead
  and the best he can do is hope it returns like a vampire
  to haunt him while he tries to fall asleep

makes him break out in a cold sweat
reaching for a hand—
no
a pen—
that was never there

It's bad to see, bad to pay attention to, anything at all.

His bed is unmade: that's bad to see. His window screen is broken: he'll get around to it. Unwashed laundry piled on his bed: just sleep under it, dear.

The indoor light is spare, miasmic, could choke a forest of mushrooms with its dimness. Pierrot works, as if for the first time, on this thing he has heard called Writing.

To be here, alone, under a tree in a field, but indoors, sitting by the dripping sink, listening to the pen scratching, as he writes,

as if to say, "I won't be giving up my ink so easily."

It's bad to see, bad to pay attention to, anything at all.

Pierrot only wears such baggy clothes for fear that, from certain vantage points,

in more form-fitting attire, he would disappear,

revealing his surreptitious two-dimensionality.

Deemed responsible for his actions, he thinks three times before he so much as speaks.

Without accountability, his world is a book of glass with ice for ink.

☆

Pierrot, of course, is the source of all his own problems:

his paranoia is the spring that draws this noxious water to the surface.

Sometimes he dreams of putting himself to sleep in the middle of crowded rooms: an act of almost coquettish defiance.

The false enthusiasm in his ear is making him nauseous. He's in a bad mood. He needs to take a step back and tell himself a different narrative:

The way out has already been provided, and it hasn't been taken.

Or there never was a way out, because it wasn't opted for.

Only he took it that way, and it wasn't his to take—not even in delusion.

☆

Running Pierrot makes swift, jerky movements, kicking his legs out in front of him with his toes pointed straight ahead, the soles of his feet parallel to the ground. When his legs are forward, his arms are held back, and vice versa. Even after a good stretch, he is unable to run in a very straight line.

☆

Pierrot has no ambition left : we've let it drain away by never asking him to share with us its fruit.

Please don't leave him more than one choice.

As night turns to day, he begins to feel the troughs of his sobriety.

☆

Pierrot was afraid of heights until, brought home from a city where it had rained for months

by some unavoidable appointment,

he dreamed of crossing the threshold of black clouds,

saw the sun shining over their topsides.

Elevation, then, became associated for him with deliverance,

especially in winter, when the clouds were at their most glacial, dispossessed of the roundness commonly associated with them :

the hinge of their symbol as lofty, silver-lined bringers of relief.

Pierrot is *just so tired* of fighting the air for that feeling of
relevance in the conversations he admires
    that the air puffing from his ears has turned to a vapor,
    and some powder, like cinnamon, has fallen from the trees
into the hollows of his male skull,
    and, wettened there by his cerebrospinal fluid,
    has turned to the ink blotting out his ambition,
    letter by letter.

Jealous Pierrot carries a stick in one hand and holds it over his
shoulder, which resembles the grip of a bindle, but which he thinks
of more as a bayonet rifle. He marches with his shoulders rising and
falling to a two-time rhythm, now counted out in triplets, like so:
clippity, clippity, clippity clop—bock, bock, bock.

☆

Pierrot doesn't want to be one of those people who cancel
dinner plans at the last minute because they're "in a mood,"
    but he is also sensitive to the possibility of his being
unpleasant company.
    In the end, he tends to stay home,

not because of his bad way or the quality of his company,

but because of the momentous anxiety brought on by his vacillation between these two possibilities

and his inability to determine which represents a more liveable excuse.

As, when urinating, Pierrot may actually consider that,

should he try to minimize the sound of his urination by aiming his stream at an angle of the porcelain slope—

thereby keeping quiet, polite—

he may not only splash the shins of his pantlegs, but,

through the sharp timbre of his flow, only glancing the water,

incur the thought, in those who chance to overhear, that his stream is weak, and so, his member equally lacking, and he, too, lacking something intrinsic,

and he may choose, more than half unwillingly, to aim for the water's center,

with its crass, bassy splashing,

for, however much he hates the distasteful sounds resounding from behind the bathroom door,

he is more concerned about the above-mentioned assumptions,

so beyond his control,

which his anxiety is sure to feed until they appear to blossom
from rumors to common knowledge
to a fundamental axiom even he takes as given
and by whose truth he is,
for some uninterrogated reason,
ruined.

Across a bay there is the body.

It oscillates between the body I dream of when I'm not dreaming of Pierrot, the body he dreams about when he's not dreaming of me.

There is a light in the mirror, but only from where I'm standing.

Do you ever get curious about what I write in this book, Pierrot?

Go get yourself a tonic if you're so anxious you've been walking into rooms and forgetting your reason for being there.

You know the two things you want and want to believe they're not contradictory.

"I'm getting used to writing again," he says.

"And I'm watching you from this stupid Hell."

☆

There's a certain kind of writer's block Pierrot encounters, which comes from his fear of saying the wrong thing, from admitting what he doesn't want me to know and, by way of this admission, creating the possibility for me to find exactly that in what he's written.

(Write the wrong word in your notebook and already it's been broadcast twice around the world.)

It makes you wonder : does his reliance on symbolic language originate not from a desire to overcome some insufficiency of language for the sake of revealing more, but from a desire to conceal? To say enough (which is to say : to not omit), and even so, to willfully obscure, in the face of his ability to write clearly?

It's too late!

He's caught himself thinking that all language is both insufficient and symbolic. And now he's thinking it's necessarily symbolic because insufficient. Worse yet : all language is both symbolic and insufficient because it's materially other than what it addresses.

It really is too late, isn't it, to turn back?

It's like he's laid a bear trap without meat in a region with no bears and didn't cover it with leaves, so no animal but himself, once he's forgotten he put it there, could ever be so stupid as to get snared in it.

Cocky Pierrot has a stride similar to, but less extreme than Big Bad Pierrot's. His spine is stiff, though not too stiff, and his legs bend 15° further at the knees. Sometimes Cocky Pierrot walks with one hand on his waist, but more often, when he lifts his legs, he thrusts his chest forward, his arms held out before his breast like a bird of prey.

Whenever he tosses a *sou* into the fountain, sees a shooting star, or finds an eyelash on his cheek, Pierrot simply wishes the word *poetry*.

He thinks of it as a workaround to the specificity of most wishes :

poeisis, the art of bringing into being, of writing, singing, travel and focus, of love, relationship, self-care, hygiene.

Vague as it is aspirational, *poetry* means very little if taken in its practical sense ; etymologically, however, he feels it upend the storied uselessness of the genre, empower it absolutely :

poeisis, no matter the circumstance.

☆

"I will always wait for you," Pierrot once said to me.

"Why, thank you, Pierrot," was my reply.

If he is still waiting for me, I hope it's light out where he is,
   that the coming night contains no corrective, but a jamb—
   a stop to ensure some lemony aroma may creep into his
bedroom to remind him of me,
   to turn his destitution into a gas, a light,
   or a pocket of air.

ACKNOWLEDGMENTS

A number of these poems appeared, some in earlier versions, in *Ancients*, *BOMB*, *Boston Review*, *Brooklyn Rail*, *Desbandada*, *ditch,*, *Elective Affinities*, *Folder*, *Hyperallergic*, *Inpatient*, *Interrupture*, *La vie manifeste*, *Stonecutter*, *Sun's Skeleton*, and the chapbooks *Journals & other Poems* (O'clock Press, 2011), *Inclusivity Blueprint* (Diez, 2015) & *The Good in Having a Nuclear Family* (Despite Editions, 2019) : grateful acknowledgment to the editors. "Proem (Skeuomorph)" was written while falling asleep and listening to a recording of Jean Day's January 2, 1988 reading for the Segue Series at the Ear Inn, and likely contains words from those poems. "Inclusivity Blueprint" contains a phrase of Keith Waldrop, although its sense has been inverted. "The Notebooks of Ana Cristina Cesar" is composed of false translations of the Brazilian poet of that name. "Metaphors We Live By" was inspired by a conversation had between Diana Hamilton, Shiv Kotecha, James Ingoldsby, and the author on July 3, 2018 in Mexico City ; its title is borrowed from the book on conceptual metaphor by George Lakoff and Mark Johnson. Raw materials for "Toward Becoming Literal" were written at the Poetry Project at St. Mark's Church while attempting and failing to transcribe by hand erica kaufman's reading, with Simone White, from her then-unpublished book, *Instant Classic* (Roof Books), on May 22, 2013; "a social appendage who is also drunk" is a coinage of Judah Rubin. The author dedicates the poem "Journals" to Robert Kelly, "Fruit Flies" to Matt Longabucco, and extends his deepest gratitude to Lynn Xu and Joshua Edwards of Canarium Books for editing and publishing this collection, his first, of poems.

Kit Schluter (Boston, 1989) is a poet-translator and book designer. His poems and short stories have appeared or are forthcoming in *Boston Review, Brooklyn Rail, BOMB, Folder, Hyperallergic,* and Wesleyan UP's *Best American Experimental Writing* anthology. Among his recent chapbooks are *The Good in Having a Nuclear Family,* as well as the English-Spanish bilingual volumes *5 Cartoons (5 caricaturas),* translated by Mariana Rodríguez, and *An Umbrella (Un paraguas),* translated by Daniel Saldaña París. His translations, published and forthcoming, include books from the French and Spanish by Amandine André, Rafael Bernal, Anne Kawala, Jaime Saenz, Michel Surya, Olivia Tapiero, Julio Torri, and three collections by Symbolist author Marcel Schwob. He holds an MFA in poetry from Brown University and is recipient of a Glascock Prize, a "Discovery"/Boston Review Prize, and a translation fellowship from the National Endowment for the Arts. Kit lives in Mexico City, where from 2017-2019 he co-organized, with Tatiana Lipkes, the translation-focused international poetry series *Salón de Belleza* at the arts library Aeromoto.